If You Give a Bunny a Beer

T0056930

If You Give a Bunny a Beer

Written by Sam Miserendino
Illustrated by Mike Odum

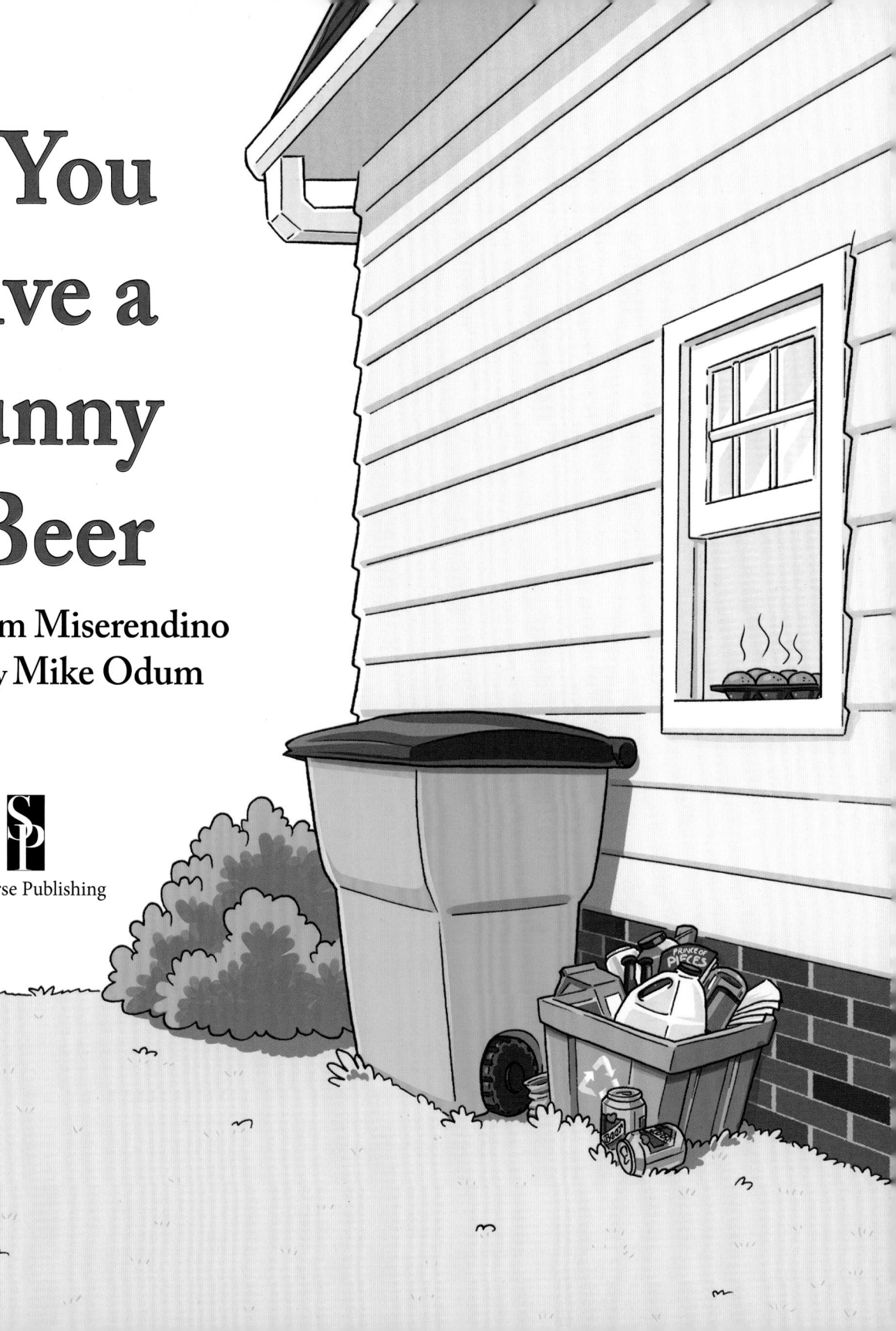

Skyhorse Publishing

Copyright © 2018 by Sam Miserendino

All rights reserved. No part of this book may be reproduced in any manner without the express written consent of the publisher, except in the case of brief excerpts in critical reviews or articles. All inquiries should be addressed to Skyhorse Publishing, 307 West 36th Street, 11th Floor, New York, NY 10018.

Skyhorse Publishing books may be purchased in bulk at special discounts for sales promotion, corporate gifts, fund-raising, or educational purposes. Special editions can also be created to specifications. For details, contact the Special Sales Department, Skyhorse Publishing, 307 West 36th Street,11th Floor, New York, NY 10018 or info@skyhorsepublishing.com.

Skyhorse® and Skyhorse Publishing® are registered trademarks of Skyhorse Publishing, Inc.®, a Delaware corporation.

Visit our website at www.skyhorsepublishing.com.

10 9 8 7 6

Library of Congress Cataloging-in-Publication Data is available on file

Cover and interior artwork by Mike Odum

Print ISBN: 978-1-5107-3395-4
eBook ISBN: 978-1-5107-3401-2

Printed in China

For Ariel and Sam
-S.M.

For Aurora
-M.O.

Special Thanks To:
Tosca Miserendino
Stacie Odum
Jeanne Miserendino
Beverly Miserendino

If you give a bunny a beer,

he'll want another.

And another…

And another…

And then he'll be
sad, because it's not fun
drinking alone.

SO...

He'll find some drinking buddies.

And they will be his
new best friends,

who understand him
better than anyone ever
has before.

When the beer
runs low...

He'll offer to make
a beer run.

He'll tell you he's
okay to drive...

Carrie

But he's not.

rie
Bean

When he sees the doll's broken arm, it will remind him of his broken heart.

And he'll start to sob...

And sob...

And sob...

Then he'll tell you about the most beautiful bunny in the world...
The only bunny he ever loved...

And how he
lost her.

And he'll sob...

And sob...

Until, through
tears and beer goggles
he sees...

HER!
A vision of beauty
that makes him forget...

Whatever it was
that he was crying
about.

He'll woo her with
poetry and wit.

He'll ask her
to dance.

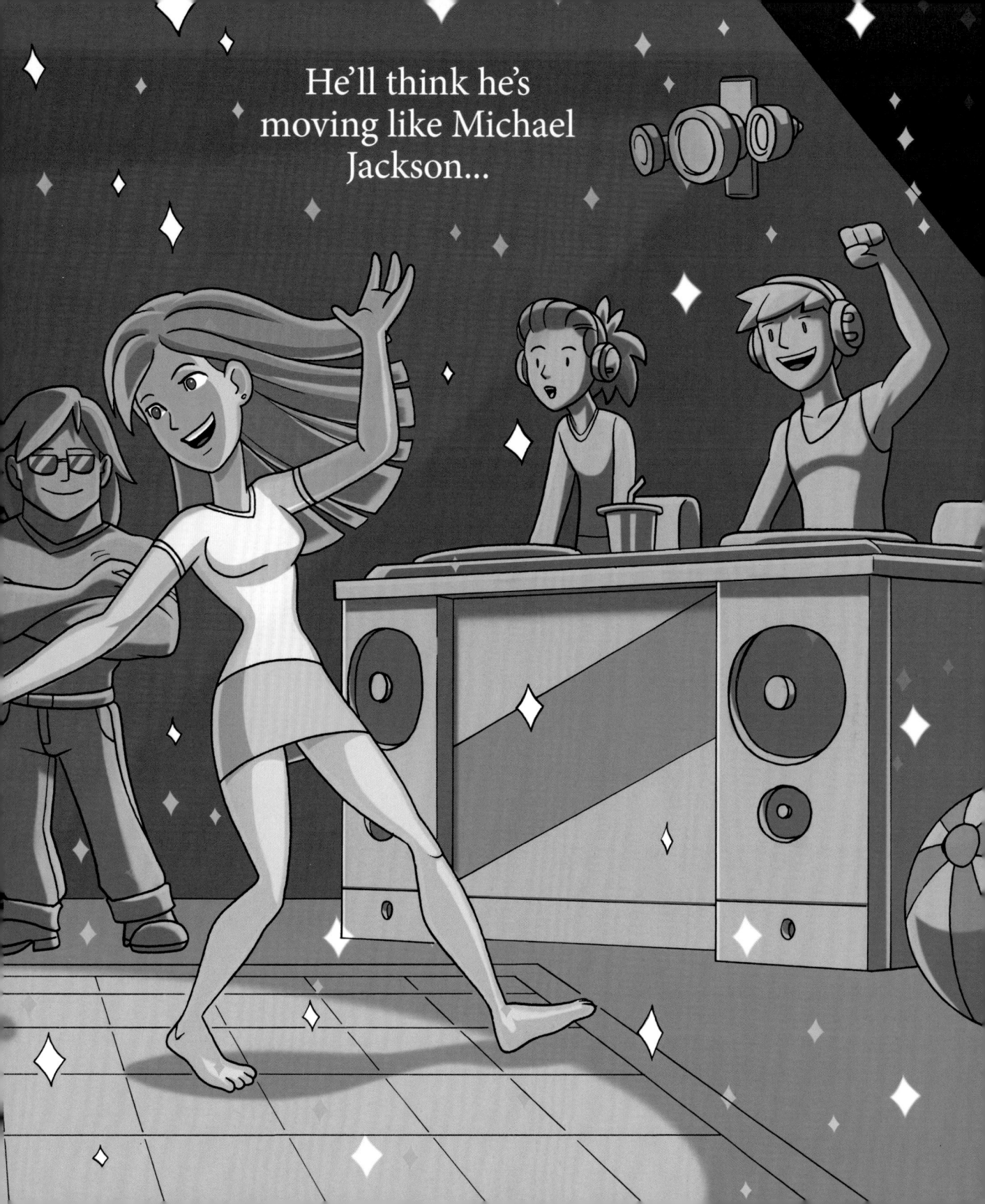
He'll think he's moving like Michael Jackson...

But he's not.

When he bumps
into someone,

beer-brain
will make him
indignant.

And beer muscles will make him fearless.

When it's over,

he'll regret that he lost his
temper. And regrets are like beer–
one leads to another...

And another...

And another...

He'll tell you what could've been...

What should've been...

If only...

If only...
Boo

He had another beer!

Another beer will make
everything clear.

He'll tell you what's wrong
with the world.

He'll tell you
what's what.

And he'll tell you...

And tell you...

Until you tell him...

IT'S TIM
TO B
Bean

E TO GO
ED!

Beer

When he's finally
in bed,

the bed will
start spinning.

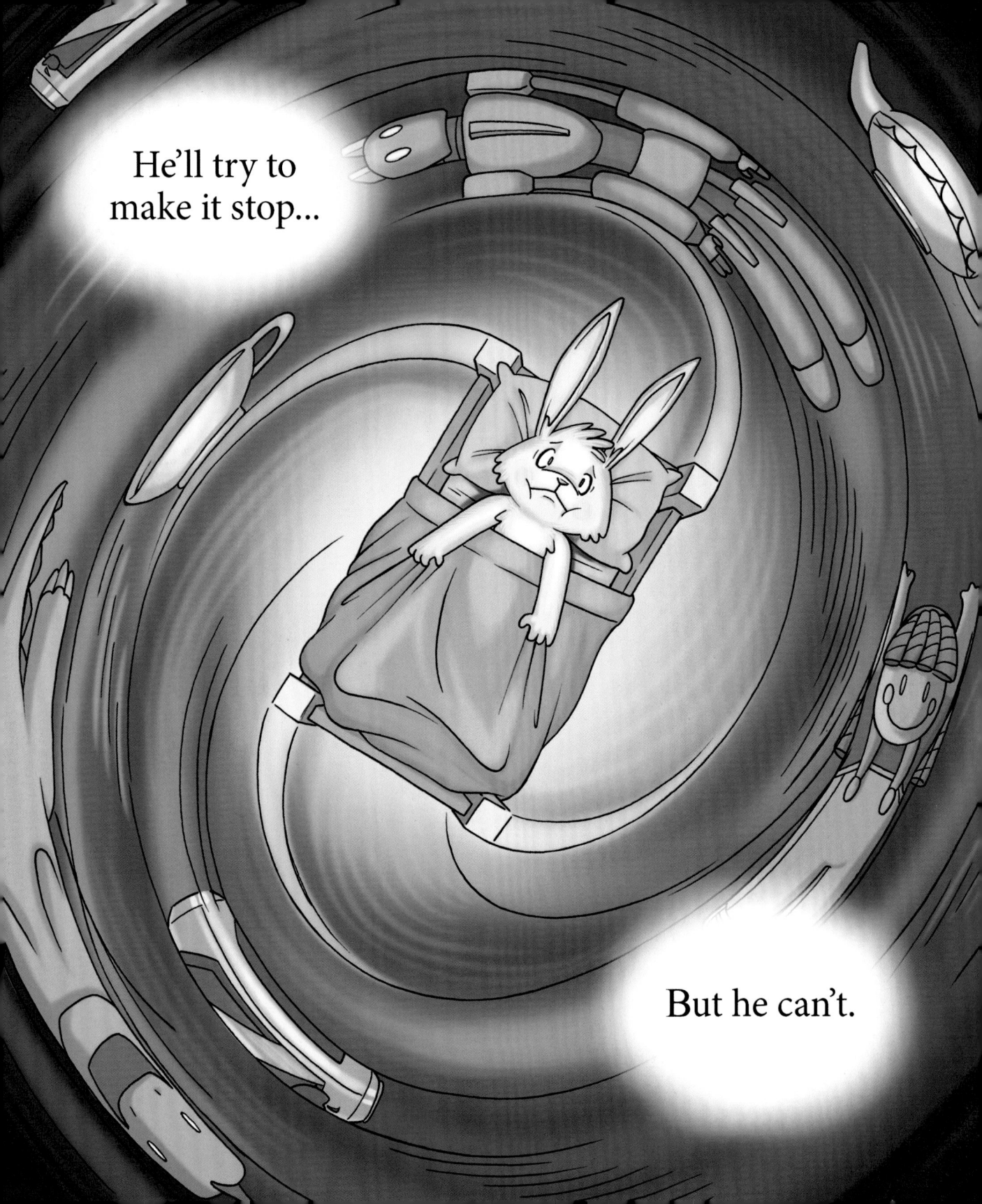
He'll try to make it stop...
But he can't.

He'll try to make it to the bathroom…

But he won't.

When he wakes up
the next morning,

he'll swear he
absolutely, positively will
never ever drink another
beer in his life...

But he will.

The End

No bunnies were harmed
in the making of this book.
One did, however, have a
really good time.